Microsoft Word 2013 Advanced

Michelle N. Halsey

ISBN-10: 1-64004-155-9

ISBN-13: 978-1-64004-155-4

Silver City Publications & Training, L.L.C.
P.O. Box 1914
Nampa, ID 83653
https://www.silvercitypublications.com/shop/

Contents

Chapter 1 – Working with the Word Window

Customizing the Word window is a powerful way to become more productive when working with documents. The first concept we will cover in this chapter is the Zoom feature, which allows you to focus in on details, or else zoom out to see the entire document. We will present an overview of the various document views available in Word. This chapter will explain how to arrange multiple windows to see more than one document at a time. We will also cover how to split a document, so that you can see more than one location in a long document at one time. You will learn some advanced uses of the Navigation pane. Finally, you will learn how to customize both the Ribbon and the Quick Access toolbar, so that your most used commands are always at your fingertips.

Using Zoom

Use the following procedure to zoom using the Status bar.

Step 1: Click the Zoom slider options to use Zoom.

- Click + to Zoom in (up to 500% of the normal view).

- Click – to Zoom out (down to 10% or small enough to see many pages at once).

- Drag the slider toward the + to zoom in or toward the – to zoom in.

- Click the current percentage to open the Zoom dialog box.

To modify and review the options of the Zoom dialog box, use the following procedure.

Step 2: To open the Zoom dialog box from the Ribbon, select the **View** Tab. Select **Zoom**.

Step 3: Select a **Zoom to** option.

- 200% is twice the print size.

- 100% is the print size.

- 75% is smaller than the print size.

- Page Width scales the view to the width of the page.

- Text Width scales the view to the width of the text.

- Whole page scales the view in order to show the whole page in one screen.

- Percent allows you to enter a precise zoom percentage. Enter a percentage or use the up and down arrows.

- Many Pages allows you to select how many pages to view in the screen. Click the arrow to select the number of pages to include.

Zoom ? ×

Zoom to
○ 200%   ○ Page width   ● Many pages:
○ 100%   ○ Text width
○ 75%   ○ Whole page

Percent: 100% ⇕

Preview

AaBbCcDdEeXxYyZz

AaBbCcDdEeXxYyZz

AaBbCcDdEeXxYyZz

AaBbCcDdEeXxYyZz

OK   Cancel

Zoom ? ×

Zoom to
○ 200%   ○ Page width   ● Many pages:
○ 100%   ○ Text width
○ 75%   ○ Whole page

Percent: 100% ⇕

Preview

Cancel   yZz

AaBbCcDdEeXxYyZz

AaBbCcDdEeXxYyZz

AaBbCcDdEeXxYyZz

OK   Cancel

Step 4: Select **OK** to apply the zoom. Or select Cancel to close the Zoom dialog box without changing the zoom.

An Overview of Word's Views

The Read Mode opens a view for reading a document on the screen. There is a minimized Ribbon with access to the Backstage View, find and search tools, and additional tools on the View tab for reading your document or switching back to editing view. To switch to Read Mode, select the **View** tab from the Ribbon. Select **Read Mode**. Or select the **Read Mode** icon from the Status Bar.

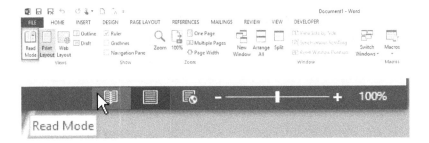

Tools available when working in Read Mode.

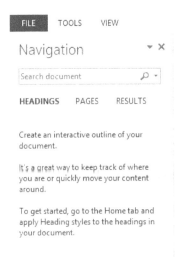

The Print Layout view makes the screen look exactly like the document will look when it prints. To switch to Print Layout view, select the **View** tab from the Ribbon. Select **Print Layout**. Or select the Print Layout icon from the Status Bar.

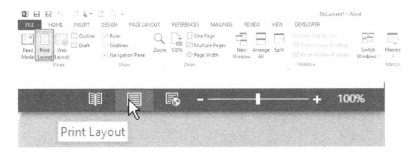

The third view available in Word 2013 is the Web Layout view. This view simulates what your document would look like on the Internet. To switch to Web Layout view, select the **View** tab from the Ribbon. Select **Web Layout**. Or select the **Web Layout** icon from the Status Bar.

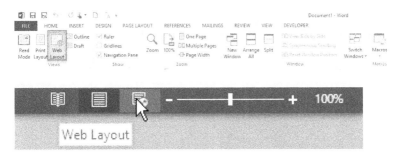

The fourth view available in Word 2013 is the Outline view. Outline view is a special view for working with levels (or paragraphs that have a Heading level style applied). This view can help you get a handle on the structure and organization of your document.

To switch to Outline view, select the **View** tab from the Ribbon. Select **Outline**.

Take a moment to review the Outline tools. A sample is illustrated below.

The fifth view available in Word 2013 is the Draft view. Draft view removes all extra white space (such as margins) and pictures. Draft view allows you to scroll much more quickly through a long document. It also allows you to see more on the screen at one time without having to adjust the zoom too small. To switch to Draft view, select the **View** tab from the Ribbon. Select **Draft**.

Arranging Windows

To arrange open windows, use the following procedure.

Step 1: Make sure all of the windows you want to view are open.

Step 2: Select the **View** tab from the Ribbon. Select **Arrange All**.

Word resizes the windows to each take a percentage of the screen; depending on how many documents you have open. The original document is on top.

Select the **Maximize** icon from the top right corner of one of the windows to return the window to its previous size and position.

Splitting a Document

To split the view, use the following procedure.

Step 1: Select the **View** tab from the Ribbon. Select **Split**.

Step 2: Word splits the view into two windows. You can drag the resize line to make one window smaller or larger.

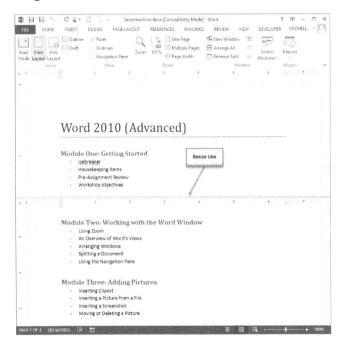

Step 3: The two windows include separate rulers and scroll bars, but not a separate Ribbon. Place your cursor in the appropriate window to apply a command to that section of the document. All the commands will work in either window.

Step 4: To remove the split, select the **View** window from the Ribbon. Select **Remove Split**.

Using the Navigation Pane

To open the Navigation pane, use the following procedure.

Step 1: Select the **View** tab from the Ribbon. Check the **Navigation Pane** box.

To navigate to another section using the Navigation pane, use the following procedure.

Step 2: Click a heading to go to that section of the document.

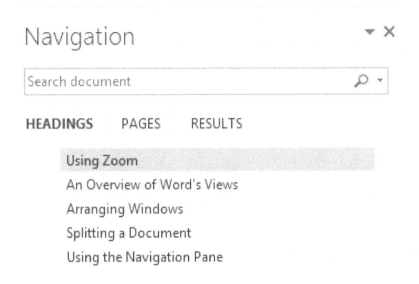

To rearrange the sections in a document using the Navigation pane, use the following procedure.

Step 3: Click a heading in the Navigation pane and drag it to the new location.

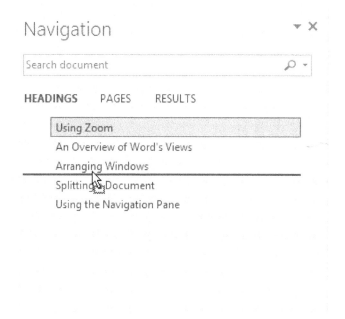

To review the options and settings in the Navigation pane context menu, use the following procedure.

Step 1: Right click a section heading in the Navigation pane to see the context menu.

Customizing the Ribbon and the Quick Access Toolbar

To customize the Ribbon, use the following procedure.

Step 1: Select the **File** tab from the Ribbon to open the Backstage View.

Step 2: Select **Options**.

Step 3: Select **Customize Ribbon** from the left side.

In the left column, under **Choose Commands From**, Word lists the commands available in the application. You can choose a different option from the **Choose Commands From** drop down list to change which options are shown or how they are sorted.

The right column shows the available tabs on the Ribbon.

Step 1: To customize the Ribbon, select the command that you want to change on the left column. Select **Add**. You may need to create a Custom Group before you can add a command.

- Select the Tab where you want the group to appear.

- Select **New Group**.

- Enter the Group name.

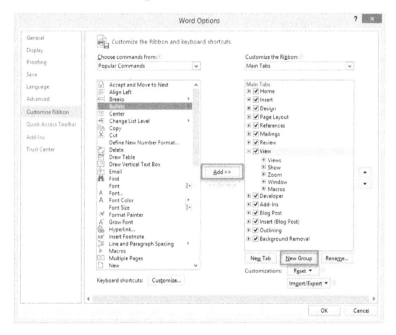

You can also remove commands or rearrange them on the right column.

When you have finished, select **OK**.

The procedure is similar when adding a command to the Quick Access Toolbar, except that you do not need to add a custom group for commands.

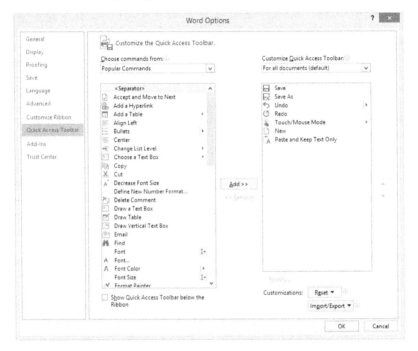

Chapter 2 – Advanced Editing and Formatting Tasks

This chapter will help you understand some more sophisticated tools to format your text, such as the character borders and shading, enclosing characters, and text effects and typography options. You will also learn how to use the phonetic guide to help you readers with pronunciation. First, we will start off with introducing the Office Clipboard to help you with multiple copy and paste tasks.

Using the Office Clipboard

To open the Clipboard Task pane, use the following procedure.

Step 1: The Home tab of the Ribbon, select the icon next to Clipboard.

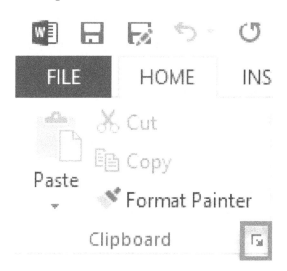

The Clipboard pane opens, displaying any items you have cut or copied in this Word 2013 session (or the 24 most recent). A sample is illustrated below.

To paste using the Office Clipboard Task pane, use the following procedure.

Step 1: Place the cursor where you want to paste text from the clipboard.

Step 2: Click the item in the Clipboard task pane that you want to paste.

Using the Phonetic Guide

To use the Phonetic Guide, use the following procedure.

Step 1: Highlight the word that you want to enhance using the Phonetic Guide.

Step 2: Select the Phonetic Guide icon from the Font group on the Home tab of the Ribbon.

Step 3: Enter (or paste) the Ruby text.

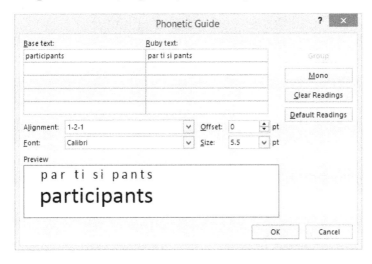

Step 4: There are additional options to change the ruby text alignment, offset, font, and size. You can group the word or illustrate the pronunciation using Mono to separate the letters.

Step 5: Select **OK** when you have finished. The word is highlighted in the document with the ruby text above.

Using Zoom

par ti si pants
Show the participants how to zoom using

Using Character Borders and Shading

Use the following procedure to apply borders or shading to text.

Step 1: Select the text that you want to enhance.

Step 2: Select the Character Border tool or the Character Shading Tool.

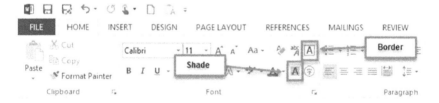

The following example has both borders and shading applied to the selected text.

Using Zoom

Show the participants how to zoom using the

Enclosing Characters

To enclose characters, use the following procedure.

Step 1: Select the character that you want to enhance.

Step 2: Select the **Enclose Characters** command from the Font group on the **Home** tab of the Ribbon.

Step 3: In the *Enclose Characters* dialog box, select the **Style** of symbol you want to use.

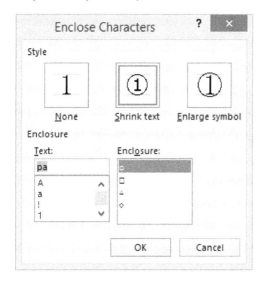

Step 4: The character you selected is the default option under **Text**. You can select another item from the list, if desired.

Step 5: Select the type of **Enclose** from the list.

Step 6: Select **OK**.

Using Text Effects

To apply text effects or typography options, use the following procedure.

Step 1: Select the text that you want to enhance.

Step 2: Select the Text effects command from the Font group on the Home tab of the Ribbon.

Step 3: Select the option that you want to use.

Chapter 3 – Working with Illustrations

This chapter will help you learn how to insert and work with pictures and other illustrations in your document. We will cover pictures from files as well as online pictures, WordArt, shapes, and screenshots. You will also learn how to move and delete the illustrations.

Inserting a Picture from a File

To insert a picture from a file, use the following procedure.

Step 1: Select the **Insert** tab from the Ribbon.

Step 2: Select **Picture**.

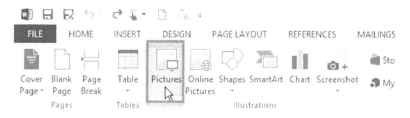

Step 3: Navigate to the location of the file and highlight the file you want to insert.

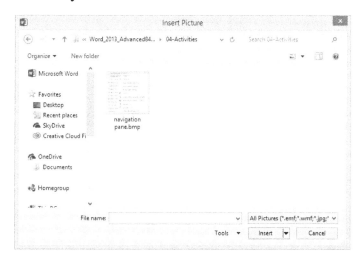

Step 4: Select **Insert**.

Word inserts the picture.

Inserting an Online Picture

To insert a clip art, use the following procedure.

Step 1: Select the **Insert** tab from the Ribbon.

Step 2: Select **Online Pictures**.

Step 3: In the *Insert Pictures* dialog box, select the place where you want to search for images.

Step 4: Enter a search term. Press Enter to begin searching.

Step 5: Word displays the matching images. To insert one, double-click it or highlight it and select **Insert**.

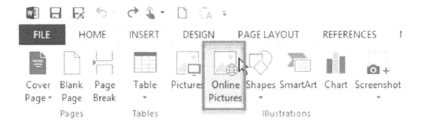

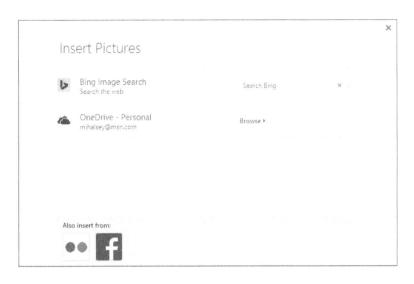

Adding WordArt

To insert WordArt, use the following procedure.

Step 1: Select the **Insert** tab from the Ribbon.

Step 2: Select **WordArt**.

Step 3: Select the style you would like to use.

Step 4: Word inserts the text box with the placeholder text highlighted. Enter your own text to replace the placeholder text.

Notice the icon to the right of the text box. Click it to see your layout options.

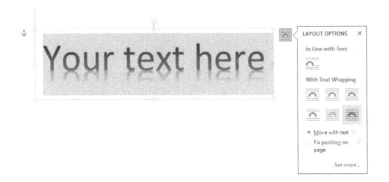

Drawing Shapes

To insert a built-in shape, use the following procedure.

Step 1: Select the **Insert** tab from the Ribbon.

Step 2: Select **Shapes**.

Step 3: Select the shape that you want to use.

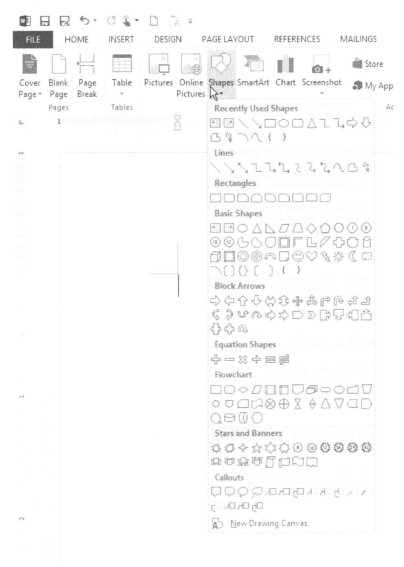

Step 4: Hold down the mouse button from the location in the document where you want to place the top left of the shape. Drag down and to the right it until the shape is the desired shape and size. The cursor changes to a cross while you are drawing.

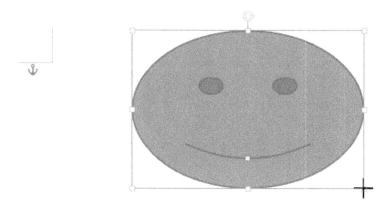

To draw with one of the freehand shapes, use the following procedure

Step 1: Select the **Insert** tab from the Ribbon.

Step 2: Select **Shapes**.

Step 3: The freehand drawing tools are in the Lines section. Select either the closed freehand shape (Freeform) or the open freehand shape (Scribble).

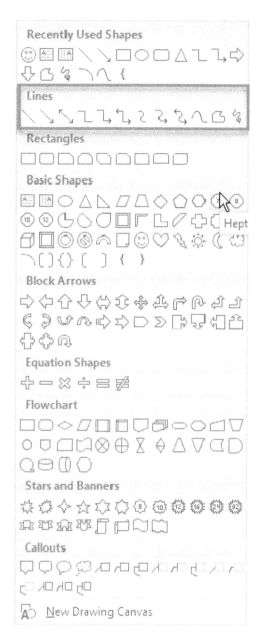

Step 4: Begin drawing. If you are using the Freeform tool, Word will close the shape when you click close to your starting point. If you are using the Scribble tool,

Word will finish the shape when you stop dragging the mouse.

Inserting a Screenshot

To insert a full size screenshot, use the following procedure.

Step 1: Select the **Insert** tab from the Ribbon.

Step 2: Select **Screenshot**.

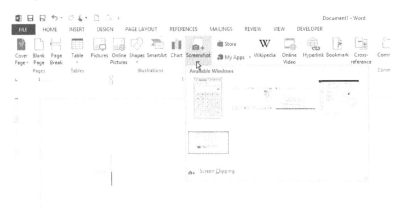

Step 3: The Screenshot gallery includes a thumbnail image of other windows you have open. Select the image that you want to insert.

Word inserts the image and may scale it to the width of your document.

To insert a screen clipping, use the following procedure.

Step 1: Make sure that the area of the screen you want in your document is ready to capture. Word will automatically return to the previous window for a screen clipping.

Step 2: Select the **Insert** tab from the Ribbon.

Step 3: Select **Screenshot**.

Step 4: Select **Screen Clipping**.

Step 5: Drag the mouse to capture the area of the screen that you want to insert in your presentation. The screen is slightly greyed out, except for the area you are capturing.

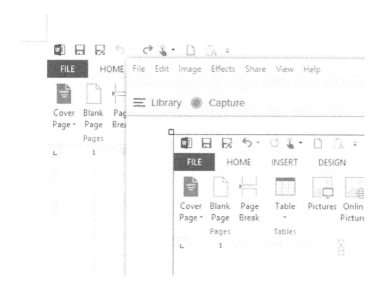

Step 6: When you release your mouse, Word inserts the screen clipping into the document at the current cursor position.

Moving or Deleting a Picture

To move a picture, use the following procedure.

Step 1: Select the picture you want to move.

The cursor changes to a cross with four arrows.

Step 2: Drag the mouse until the picture is in the desired location. Word displays a small rectangle by the cursor to show an object is being moved. There is a small line showing where the picture will be moved.

Release the mouse to drop the picture in the new location.

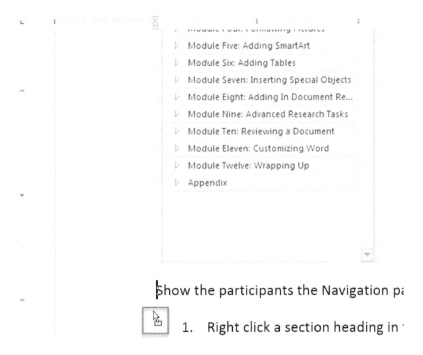

Show the participants the Navigation pa

1. Right click a section heading in

To delete a picture, use the following procedure.

Step 1: Select the picture you want to delete.

Step 2: Press the Delete key on the keyboard.

Chapter 4 – Formatting Pictures

In this chapter, you will learn how to use the Picture Tools tab. Removing a picture's background is a great technique to add professionalism to your documents. You will also learn how to add a border to a picture. This chapter also explains how to add artistic effects and change a picture's position and text wrapping. You will also learn how to use the selection pane for selecting an object when multiple objects are layered.

Using the Picture Tools Tab

To use the Picture Tools tab, use the following procedure.

Step 1: With a picture selected on the document, select the **Picture Tools/Format** tab from the Ribbon. You can use the other tabs while working with a picture, and this tab will still be available.

Adding a Border

To add a border to a picture, use the following procedure.

Step 1: Select the picture to which you want to add a border.

Step 2: Select the **Picture Tools/Format** tab from the Ribbon.

Step 3: Select **Picture Border**.

Step 4: Select a color from the gallery to use or select **More Outline Colors** to choose a **Standard** or **Custom** color as you've seen in other Word color galleries.

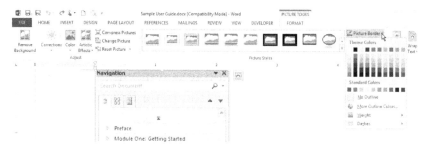

Step 5: Select **Picture Border** again to select a line weight. Select **Weight**. Select the point size line you want to use. Remember that you can preview the border for selecting it by hovering your mouse over that option.

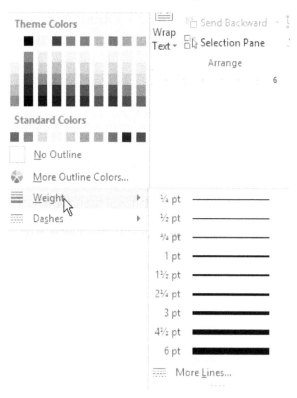

Step 6: Select **Picture Border** again to select a line style. Select **Dashes**. Select the line style you want to use.

Removing a Picture's Background

To remove the background from a picture, use the following procedure.

Step 1: Select the picture you want to change.

Step 2: On the **Picture Tools** tab of the Ribbon, select **Remove Background**.

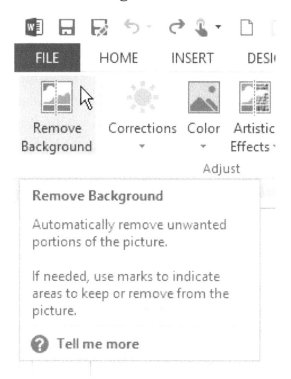

Word displays the **Background Removal** tab.

Step 3: You can drag the marquee to adjust the picture, if necessary.

Step 4: Select **Keep Changes** to accept Word's automatic background removal. Or use the **Mark Areas to Keep** or **Mark Areas to Remove** tools to refine the background removal. When you have finished, select **Keep Changes**. Or select **Discard All Changes** to return to the original picture.

Adding Artistic Effects

To add artistic effects to a picture, use the following procedure.

Step 1: Select the picture you want to change.

Step 2: On the **Picture Tools** tab of the Ribbon, select **Artistic Effects**.

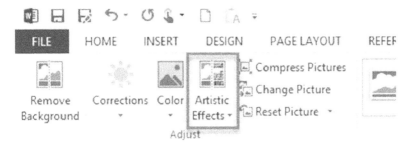

Step 3: Select the effect you would like to apply.

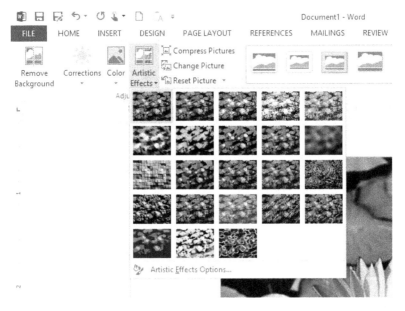

The Artistic Options in the *Format Picture* pane.

Step 1: Select **Artistic Effects Options** from the Artistic Effects gallery.

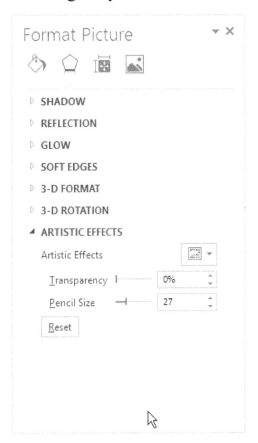

Step 2: Select the **Artistic Effect** from the drop down list.

Step 3: Depending on which effect you select, there are different options to adjust, such as transparency, pressure, or brush size. Use the up and down arrows or enter the amounts for each option.

Step 4: Select the **Reset** button to return to the default settings for the selected option.

Positioning Pictures and Wrapping Text

To set the positioning for a picture, use the following procedure.

Step 1: Select the picture you want to change.

Step 2: On the **Picture Tools** tab of the Ribbon, select **Position**.

Step 3: Select the Position that you want to use. You can use the Layout dialog box to refine it later, if needed.

Use the following procedure to set the text wrapping for a picture.

Step 1: Select the picture you want to change.

Step 2: On the **Picture Tools** tab of the Ribbon, select **Wrap Text**.

Step 3: Select the wrapping option that you want to use. You can use the Layout dialog box to refine it later, if needed.

The purpose of a newsletter is to provide specialized information to a targeted audience. Newsletters can be a great way to communicate with family and friends on a regular basis.

You can tell stories about your life, your children's activities, your vacations or travel plans, new pets, or whatever you want to tell those closest to you! You can add pictures, too.

You can also find interesting articles and information for your friends to read by accessing the World Wide Web.

Much of the content you put in your newsletter can also be used for your Web site. Microsoft Word offers a simple way to convert your newsletter to a Web publication. So, when you're finished writing your newsletter, convert it to a Web site and post it.

The purpose of a newsletter is to provide specialized information to a targeted audience. Newsletters can be a great way to communicate with family and friends on a regular basis.

You can tell stories about your life, your children's activities, your vacations or travel plans, new pets, or whatever you want to tell those closest to you! You can add pictures, too.

Use the following procedure to use the Layout dialog box.

Step 1: Select the picture you want to change.

Step 2: On the **Picture Tools** tab of the Ribbon, select EITHER **Wrap Text** or **Position**.

Step 3: Select **More Layout Options**.

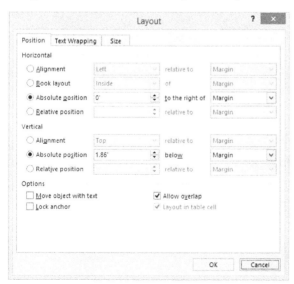

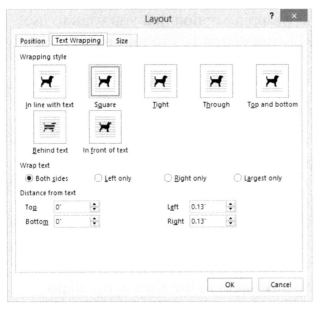

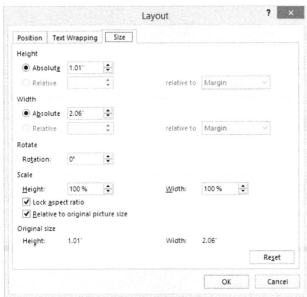

48

Using the Selection Pane

To open the selection pane, use the following procedure.

Step 1: Select any object on the page to access the **Picture Tools Format** tab on the Ribbon.

Step 2: Select the **Selection Pane** tool.

Step 3: In the *Selection Pane*, you can rename the objects by clicking on an item and entering a new name. You can also use the Send Forward and Send Backward arrow icons to reorder the objects. The Show all and Hide all allow you to hide from the editing view all of the objects or show them all again. You can show or hide individual objects by clicking on the eye next to the name for that object.

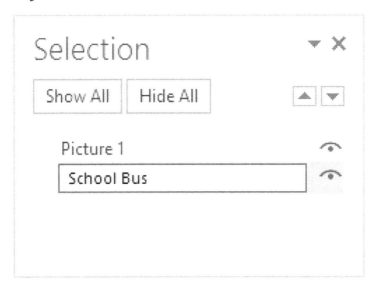

Chapter 5 – Adding SmartArt

This chapter will show you how to add SmartArt graphics anywhere in your document. You will learn more about the SmartArt Tools tabs, and how to add text to a SmartArt graphic. You will also learn how to move and delete SmartArt graphics. Finally, we will look at the SmartArt Layout options.

Inserting SmartArt

To insert SmartArt, use the following procedure.

Step 1: Select the **Insert** tab from the Ribbon.

Step 2: Select **SmartArt**.

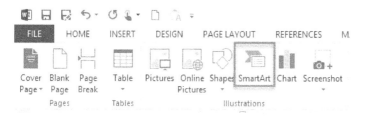

Step 3: In the *Choose a SmartArt Graphic* dialog box, select the category on the left. Then you select the item in the middle. The right shows a preview of the item. Select **OK** to insert the content.

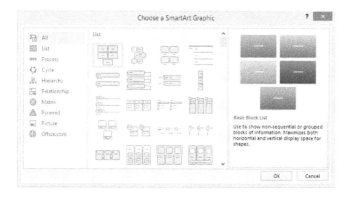

Word inserts the selected SmartArt graphic in the document at the current cursor position.

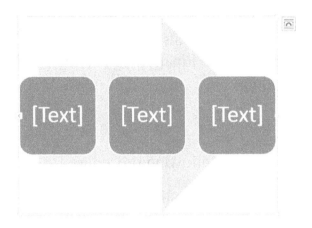

Adding Text to SmartArt

To add text to a SmartArt graphic by using the Text Pane, use the following procedure.

Step 1: To the left of the SmartArt graphic you inserted, there is a small rectangle with an arrow. Click this arrow to open the Text Pane.

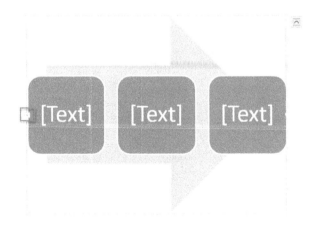

Word opens the Text Pane.

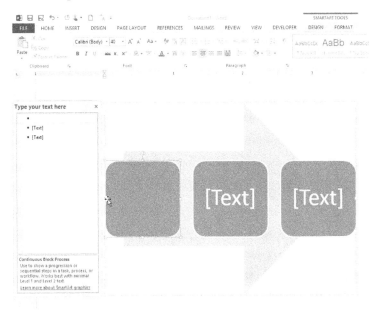

Step 2: Click the first line and begin typing. Each line represents a new item in the graphic.

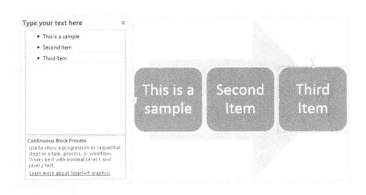

The SmartArt text adjusts to fit the graphic. The more text you enter in each graphic element, the smaller the text will become.

Step 3: When you have finished, click anywhere on the slide, and the Text Pane will close automatically. Or you can click the X in the top right corner.

Using the SmartArt Tools Tabs

Use the following procedure to use the Tools tabs for working with SmartArt.

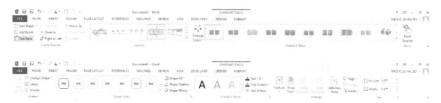

In the **Design** tab, the Create Graphic tools allow you to customize the SmartArt by adding a shape, adding a bullet point, promoting and demoting or moving a shape right to left, moving a shape up or down and changing the layout. You can also open the Text pane. The change colors option allows you to use the same graphic with different colors.

The reset graphic option removes any changes you have made and returns the selected SmartArt graphic to the default settings. It does not remove your text.

In the Format tab, the tools specific to Smart art allow you to change a selected shape or make it smaller or larger.

Moving and Deleting SmartArt

To move the diagram, use the following procedure.

Step 1: Select the diagram border.

The cursor changes to a cross with four arrows.

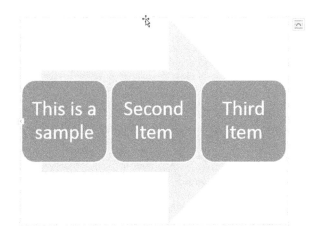

Step 2: Drag the mouse to the desired location. Word displays a small rectangle by the cursor to show an object is being moved. There is a small line showing where the diagram will be moved. Release the mouse to drop the diagram in the new location.

Using SmartArt Layout and Style Options

To change the SmartArt layout, use the following procedure.

Step 1: Select the SmartArt graphic you want to change.

Step 2: On the SmartArt Tools Design tab of the Ribbon, select the down arrow next to the Layout group to see the Layout options.

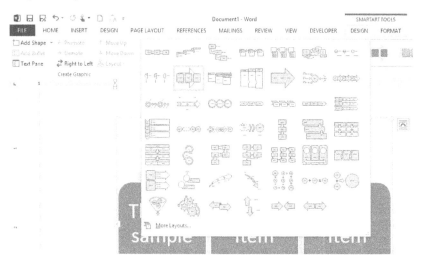

Step 3: Select the layout you would like to apply.

Step 4: To change the style, select the arrow next to the Style group too see the options. Select the style that you would like to apply.

Chapter 6 – Adding Tables

This chapter will explain how to work with tables. You will learn how to add tables to your document and add text to the table. You will also learn about the Table Tools tab. This chapter explains how to modify rows and columns and how to format a table, so that it looks just like you want it to. Finally, you will learn about Quick tables, an easy way to get a table that is already formatted into your document.

Inserting a Table

To insert a table, use the following procedure.

Step 1: Select the **Insert** tab from the Ribbon.

Step 2: Select **Table**.

Step 3: Highlight the number of rows and columns that you want to insert.

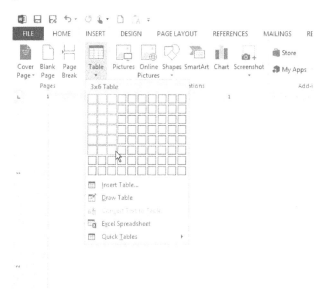

Word inserts the table in the document at the current cursor position. You can also see a preview before you insert the table.

Adding Text to a Table

To add text to a table, use the following procedure.

Step 1: Click the table cell you want to change.

Step 2: Begin typing.

Step 3: To enter text in another cell, click that cell.

Sample Header	Sample Header 2	Sample Header 3
Sample Text	Column 2	Column 3

About the Table Tools Tabs

The following diagrams show the Tools tabs for working with tables.

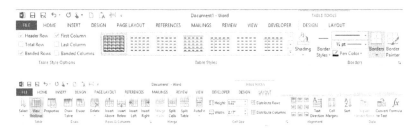

The Design tab has several options to help you apply style to your table, including borders and shading. The Layout tab has other tools to modify your table.

We will investigate many of these options in the rest of this chapter.

To modify rows and columns, use the following procedure.

Step 1: Hover your mouse over a row or column divider. The mouse changes to a divider with arrows pointing to the left and to the right.

Sample Header	Sample Header 2	Sample Header 3
Sample Text	Column 2	Column 3

Step 2: Drag the column to the new size.

Sample Header	Sample Header 2	Sample Header 3
Sample Text	Column 2	Column 3

To insert a row, use the following procedure.

Step 1: Select the row below where you want the new row to appear.

Step 2: Make sure that the **Table Tools/Layout** tab is selected.

Step 3: Select **Insert Above**.

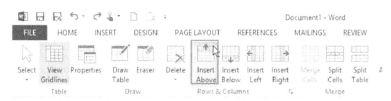

Word inserts the new row.

Sample Header	Sample Header 2	Sample Header 3
Sample Text	Column 2	Column 3

To delete a column, use the following procedure.

Step 1: Select the column you want to delete.

Step 2: Make sure that the **Table Tools/Layout** tab is selected.

Step 3: Select **Delete**.

Step 4: Select **Delete Columns**.

Applying a Table Style

To format a table, use the following procedure.

Step 1: Select the table you want to format.

Step 2: Use the Table Style options to add special formatting to the Header Row, Total Row (last row), First Column, or Last Column. The Banded Rows and Banded Columns alternate the shading.

Step 3: Select a Table style to create a new look for the table. You can see a preview by hovering the mouse over the option before selecting it.

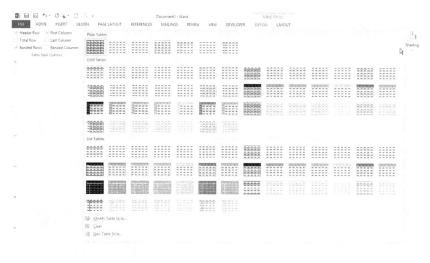

About Quick Tables

To insert a Quick Table, use the following procedure.

Step 1: Select the **Insert** tab from the Ribbon.

Step 2: Select **Table**.

Step 3: Select **Quick Tables**.

Step 4: Select the table you want to insert.

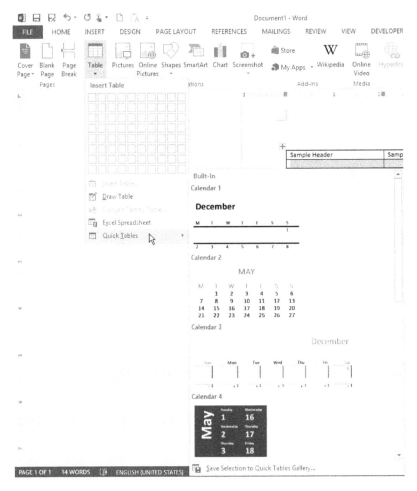

To save a table as a Quick Table selection, use the following procedure.

Step 1: Highlight the table that you have inserted and customized.

Step 2: Select the **Insert** tab from the Ribbon.

Step 3: Select **Table**.

Step 4: Select **Quick Tables**.

Step 5: Select **Save Selection to Quick Tables Gallery**.

Word displays the *Create New Building Block* dialog box.

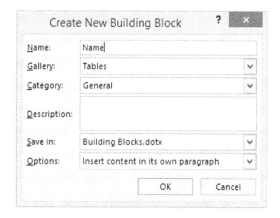

Step 6: Enter a name for the table or leave the default heading.

Step 7: Select **OK** to save the table.

Chapter 7 – Inserting Special Objects

This chapter will explain how to work with other objects to enhance your documents even further. You will learn how to add a cover page and text boxes to your document. You will also learn about the new features in 2013 to insert an app or online media. Finally, you will learn how to insert the data from a database, using Query Options and Table AutoFormat options.

Adding a Cover Page

To insert a cover page, use the following procedure.

Step 1: Select the **Insert** tab from the Ribbon.

Step 2: Select **Cover Page**.

Step 3: Select an option from the Cover Page gallery.

Word inserts the cover page.

Step 4: For each of the elements on the page, click the field and enter the new text. For example, in the above illustration, when you click anywhere on [Type the document title], the entire field is selected. Begin typing to enter the Title.

Inserting a Text Box

To insert a text box, use the following procedure.

Step 1: Place your cursor where you want the text box to appear in the document. Some built-in styles appear to the left or right. However, all text boxes have an anchor somewhere in the text of the document.

Step 2: Select the **Insert** tab from the Ribbon.

Step 3: Select **Text Box**.

Step 4: Select one of the text box gallery objects, or select Draw Text box.

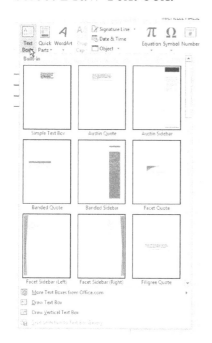

Word inserts the text box. If you selected Draw Text Box, draw the text box just like a shape.

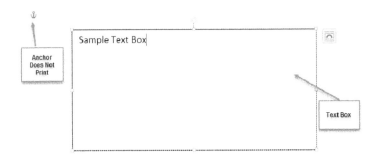

Step 5: Enter your text.

Inserting an App

To get an app for Office 2013, use the following procedure.

Step 1: Select the **Insert** tab from the Ribbon.

Step 2: Select **Apps for Office**.

Step 3: Select **See All**.

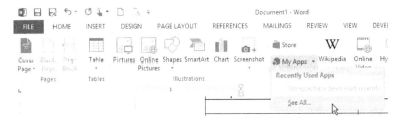

Step 4: The *Insert App* dialog box allows you to search or browse for available apps.

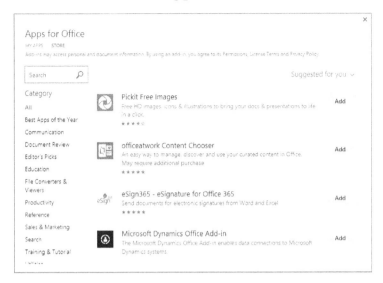

The **Manage My Apps** option in the *Insert App* dialog box opens the Office Store for your account, where you can see apps that you have installed or tried.

Step 5: When you click the App name in the *Insert App* dialog box, a task pane opens on the right side of the Word window. You can begin using the app immediately.

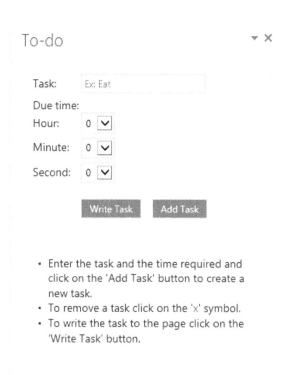

- Enter the task and the time required and click on the 'Add Task' button to create a new task.
- To remove a task click on the 'x' symbol.
- To write the task to the page click on the 'Write Task' button.

Inserting Online Media

To insert online media, use the following procedure.

Step 1: Select the **Insert** tab from the Ribbon.

Step 2: Select **Online Video**.

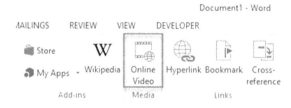

Step 3: In the *Insert Video* dialog box, enter a search term in the **Bing Video Search** field. Or enter the **Video Embed Code** from a web site.

Insert Video

Bing Video Search
Search the web

YouTube
The largest worldwide video-sharing community!

Search YouTube

From a Video Embed Code
Paste the embed code to insert a video from a web site

Paste embed code here

Step 4: If you entered a search term, Word displays videos that match your search term. Select the video that you want to use, and select **Insert**.

‹ BACK TO SITES

Bing Video Search
677000 search results for business meeting

business meeting

Select an item.   Insert   Cancel

Step 5: Word inserts the video into the document.

Inserting a Database

To insert data from a database into the document, use the following procedure.

Step 1: Select the **Insert** tab from the Ribbon.

Step 2: Select **Insert Database**.

Step 3: In the *Database* dialog box, select **Get Data**.

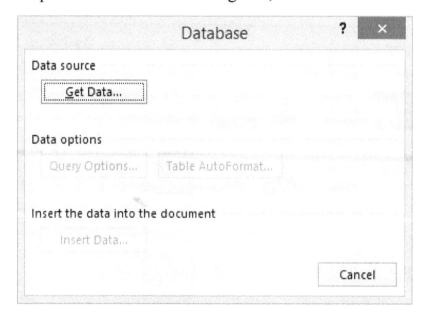

Step 4: Navigate to the location of the database file you want to use. Highlight and select **Open**.

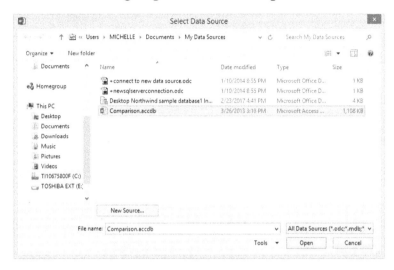

Step 5: If your database includes more than one table, the *Select Table* dialog box is displayed. Select the table that you want to use and select **OK**.

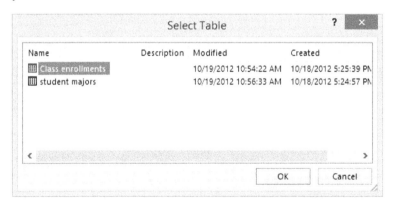

Step 6: You can use a query to narrow the data that you insert into your document. Select **Query Options** from the Database dialog box.

Step 6a: The **Filter Records** tab allows you to select a **Field**, a **Comparison term**, and the details for the filter.

Step 6b: The **Sort Records** tab allows you to select how to sort the data.

Step 6c: The **Select Fields** tab allows you to choose which fields to show.

Step 6d: Select **OK** when you have finished setting your Query Options.

Step 7: You can use an automatic format for the table Word will insert. Select **Table AutoFormat**. You can choose a **Format** and see a **Preview**. The checkboxes allow you to choose which formats and special formats to apply to your table. Select **OK** when you have finished.

Step 8: The *Insert Data* dialog box allows you to choose all records or from a select set. To choose a select set, enter the **Start** and **End** records. You can choose to insert data as a Word field. Select **OK**.

Step 9: Word inserts the data as a table.

ID	Student ID	Year	Term	Curriculum	Course No	Grade
14	135791357	2005	3	ARTH	112	A
17	147025836	2005	3	BIOL	113	B
18	147025836	2005	3	CHEM	113	B
2	123456789	2005	3	ENGL	101	B
5	223334444	2005	3	ENGL	112	A
8	223334444	2005	1	ENGL	201	B
13	135791357	2005	3	HIST	102	A
3	123456789	2005	1	MATH	242	C
4	123456789	2005	1	MATH	224	C
6	223334444	2005	3	MATH	120	C
9	987654321	2005	3	MATH	120	A
1	123456789	2005	3	MATH	221	A
12	987654321	2005	1	MATH	242	C
24	707070707	2005	1	MATH	224	C
15	135791357	2005	1	MATH	120	B
16	135791357	2005	1	MATH	141	C
19	147025836	2005	1	MATH	120	D
21	707070707	2005	3	MATH	221	B
23	707070707	2005	1	MATH	242	D
11	987654321	2005	1	MATH	221	B
7	223334444	2005	1	POSC	110	A

Chapter 8 – Working with Document References

This chapter explains how to use Word's reference tools. First, we will discuss how to add a caption to an illustration. You can add an automatically generated table of contents. Word makes it easy to add footnotes, endnotes, and other citations. Once you have added references, the Manage Sources tool helps you to keep track of those sources, which can be especially helpful in a long document or when sharing references across multiple documents. This chapter will explain how to insert a bibliography. We will end with a discussion on creating an index.

Inserting a Caption

To add a caption, use the following procedure.

Step 1: Select the **References** tab from the Ribbon.

Step 2: Select **Insert Caption**.

Step 3: In the *Caption* dialog box, enter the text for your **Caption**. The Label and the Numbering are shown by default.

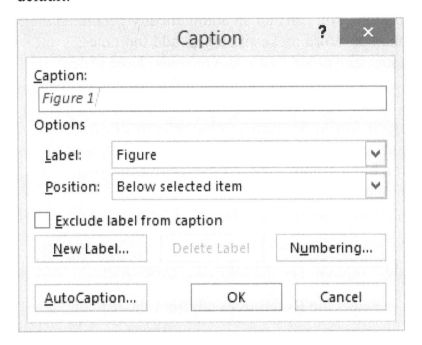

Step 4: To change the Label, select a new option from the **Label** drop down list. You can also select **New Label** to create a custom label. Just enter the text and select **OK**, and it will be added to the drop down list of options for Labels. You can select **Delete Label** to remove it from the list.

Step 5: You can select a new **Position** for the caption by selecting an item from the drop down list.

Step 6: Select **Numbering** to choose the format for the caption number.

Step 7: Select **OK** to add your Caption.

Adding a Table of Contents

To add a table of contents, use the following procedure.

Step 1: Place your cursor in the document where you want the table of contents to appear.

Step 2: Select the **References** tab from the Ribbon.

Step 3: Select **Table of Contents**.

Step 4: Select one of the built-in Table of Contents styles.

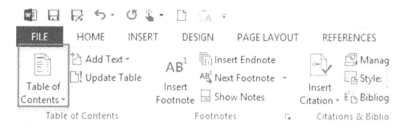

Word inserts the table of contents at the cursor.

To review the options and settings of the Table of Contents dialog box, use the following procedure.

Step 1: Select the **References** tab from the Ribbon.

Step 2: Select **Table of Contents**.

Step 3: Select **Custom Table of Contents**.

Word displays the *Table of Contents dialog box*.

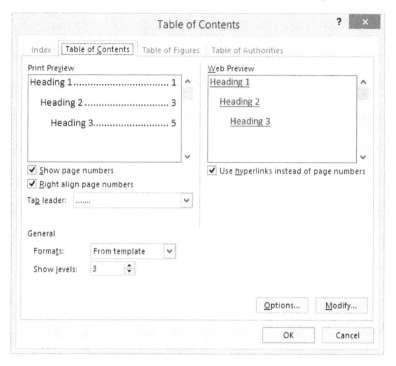

Step 4: To insert a customized table of contents, complete the Table of Contents dialog box.

- You can see a preview of your selections for box print and web distribution.

- You can select whether to show the page numbers, and what kind of tab leader to use between the headings and page numbers.

- You can select what kind of style to use and how many heading levels to include.

- Select **Options** to open the Options dialog box. Here you can indicate which paragraph styles to include in the table of contents at each TOC level. Select OK when you have finished.

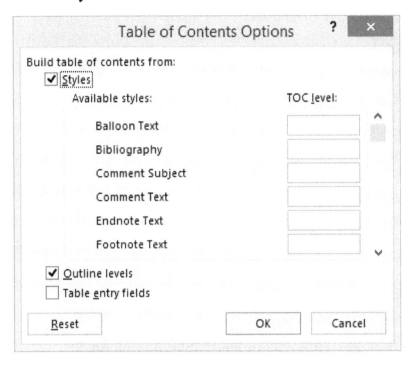

- Select **Modify** to change the appearance of the table of contents entries. Select **OK** when you have finished.

To update a table of contents, use the following procedure.

Step 1: Click anywhere on the table.

Step 2: Select the **References** tab from the Ribbon.

Step 3: Select **Update Table**.

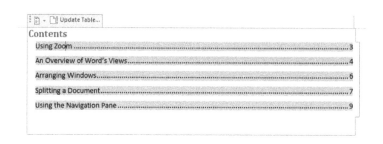

Word displays the *Update Table of Contents* dialog box.

Step 4: If the headings have changed, make sure to select Update entire table.

Step 5: Select **OK**.

Adding Footnotes, Endnotes, and Citations

To add a footnote, use the following procedure.

Step 1: Place your cursor where the notation for the footnote needs to go.

Step 2: Select the **References** tab from the Ribbon.

Step 3: Select **Insert Footnote**.

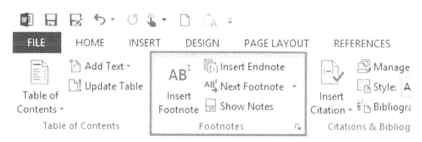

Word inserts a number at the cursor location. It is already formatted as a superscript font. Word also inserts a line and the matching number at the bottom of the page. It also places the cursor so that you can type the footnote text.

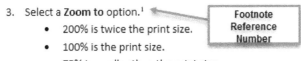

3. Select a **Zoom to** option.[1]

    Footnote Reference Number

    - 200% is twice the print size.
    - 100% is the print size.
    - 75% is smaller than the print size.
    - Page Width scales the view to the width of the page.
    - Text Width scales the view to the width of the text.

[1]
Footnote

Step 4: Begin typing the footnote text.

To add an endnote, use the following procedure.

Step 1: Place your cursor where the notation for the endnote needs to go.

Step 2: Select the **References** tab from the Ribbon.

Step 3: Select **Insert Endnote**.

Word inserts a number at the cursor location. It is already formatted as a superscript font. Word also inserts a line and the matching number at the end of the document. It also places the cursor so that you can type the endnote text.

ⁱ

ⁱⁱ Sample Endnote

To insert a citation, use the following procedure.

Step 1: Place your cursor in the paragraph that needs to be referenced.

Step 2: Select the **References** tab from the Ribbon.

Step 3: Select **Insert Citation**.

Step 4: To enter a placeholder, select **Add New Placeholder**.

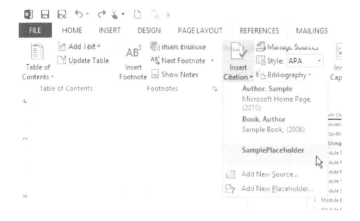

Step 5: In the *Placeholder Name* dialog box, enter a tag name to help you remember the source. The name cannot include any spaces or special characters. Select **OK**.

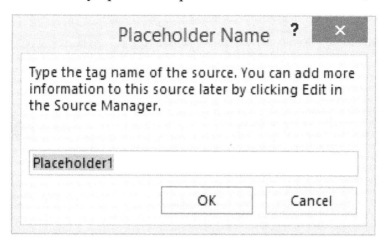

Step 6: To enter a source, select **Add New Source** from the Insert Citation command on the Ribbon. In the *Create Source* dialog box, enter the bibliography information. Select **OK**.

Managing Sources

To use the Source Manager, use the following procedure.

Step 1: Select the **References** tab from the Ribbon.

Step 2: Select **Manage Sources**.

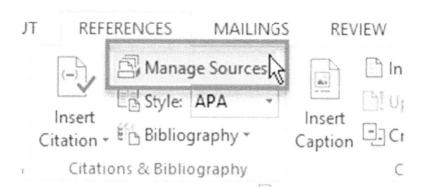

Word opens the *Source Manager* dialog box.

Explain the different areas of the Source Manager dialog box.

The **Search** fields allow you to narrow the list in the **Sources available in** area. Select the **Sort By** option from the drop down list and begin typing the name in the **Search** field. Word automatically narrows the list displayed to any matching options.

Word includes a master citation list for your computer. To open the list for another document, select **Browse**. Navigate to the location of the source file (in XML format), highlight it, and select **Open**.

The left list includes the citations in the selected citation file or the Master List. You can **Copy**, **Delete**, **Edit**, or create a **New** citation for the current list or the Master List.

- To copy a citation from one list to the other, highlight the citation and select **Copy**.

- To delete a citation in either list, highlight it and select **Delete**.

- To edit a citation, highlight it and select **Edit**. Word opens the *Edit Source* dialog box, which includes the same information as the *Create Source* dialog box from the previous topic.

- To create a new citation, select **New**. Word opens the *Create Source* dialog box.

The bottom area of the *Source Manager* dialog box displays the preview for how the currently highlighted citation will look in the bibliography.

Select **Close** when you have finished working with the sources.

Inserting a Bibliography

To insert a bibliography, use the following procedure.

Step 1: Place your cursor in the location where you want to add the bibliography.

Step 2: Select the **References** tab from the Ribbon.

Step3: Select **Bibliography**.

Step 4: Select the desired style of Bibliography from the Bibliography gallery.

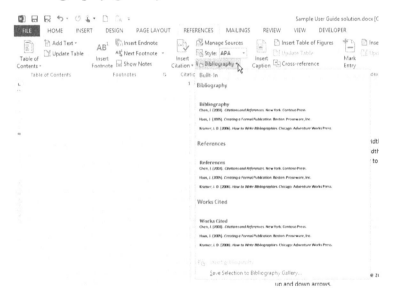

Word inserts the bibliography, including tools to change the style of the bibliography and update the citations.

Creating an Index

To mark an index entry, use the following procedure.

Step 1: If desired, highlight the text you want to include in the index from your document. Or simply place your cursor in the line where the index entry should point.

Step 2: Select the **References** tab from the Ribbon.

Step 3: Select **Mark Entry**.

Word opens the Mark Index Entry dialog box. If you highlighted text, that text appears as the Main Entry.

Step 4: Enter the text for the **Main entry** and the **subentry** (if desired).

Step 5: Select whether to refer to a **cross reference** (enter the text), the **current page**, or a **page range** (select a bookmark from the drop down list).

Step 6: Select any special formatting for the page number.

Step 7: Select **Mark** or **Mark All**.

Word inserts an index marker, which you can see if you have the paragraph markers visible. Note that these markers are not visible in the printed document.

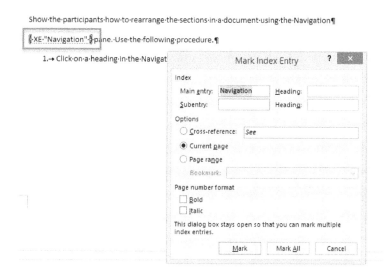

Step 8: The dialog box will stay open as long as you need it. Select **Close** when you have finished marking index entries.

To insert an index, use the following procedure.

Step 1: After you have marked at least some of your index entries, place your cursor where you want the index to appear.

Step 2: Select the **References** tab from the Ribbon.

Step 3: Select Insert Index.

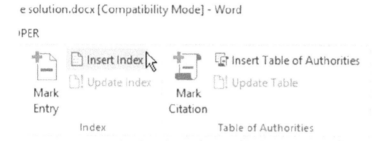

Word opens the *Index* dialog box.

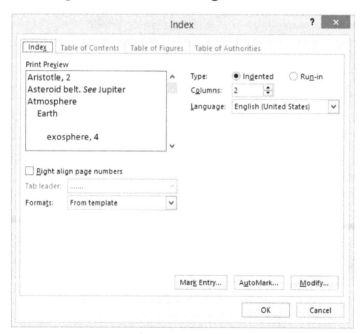

Step 4: Check the **Right align page numbers** box if desired.

Step 5: Select the **Type** as **Indented** or **Run-in**.

Step 6: Select the number of **Columns**.

Step 7: Select the **Language**.

Step 8: Select **OK**.

Word inserts the index at the current location.

¶

¶

This chapter explains how to use Word's advanced research tools. The dictionary, thesaurus and Word count tools are proofing tools that each opens a separate task pane or dialog box. The Translation tools allow you to translate a document or selected text. You can also use the mini translator to obtain a quick translation that is only temporarily visible. Finally, we will discuss the language tools to help you set your proofing language and other language preferences.

Using Define, Thesaurus and Word Count

To use the dictionary, use the following procedure.

Step 1: Highlight the word you would like to research.

Step 2: Select the **Review** tab.

Step 3: Select **Define.**

Word displays the *Dictionary* task pane (with the dictionary that you have previously installed as an app) with the word you selected defined.

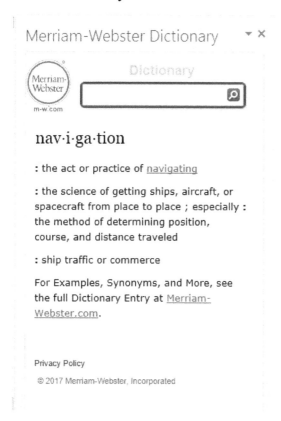

To use the thesaurus, use the following procedure.

Step 1: Highlight the word you would like to research.

Step 2: Select the **Review** tab.

Step 3: Select **Thesaurus.**

Word displays the *Thesaurus* task pane (with the dictionary that you have previously installed as an app) with the results for the word you selected displayed.

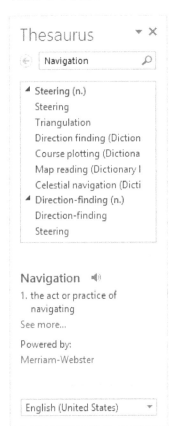

Step 4: To replace the selected word in the document with one of the words listed in the Thesaurus pane, right click the word you want to use and select **Insert** from the context menu.

In the Word Count dialog box. Note that the statistics show for selected text (if applicable) or the entire document.

Using Translation Tools

To use the Translation tools, use the following procedure.

Step 1: Select the **Review** tab.

Step 2: Select **Translate**. Select **Choose Translation Language**.

Step 3: In the *Translation Language Options* dialog box, You will select the language to use in the Mini Translator first. Below, you set the To and From languages for document translation. For all three options, select the language you want to use from the drop down list.

Step 4: Select **OK**.

Step 5: From the Review tab, select **Translate** again.

Step 5a: Select **Translate Document** to translate the entire document. The text opens in Internet Explorer using an online translation service.

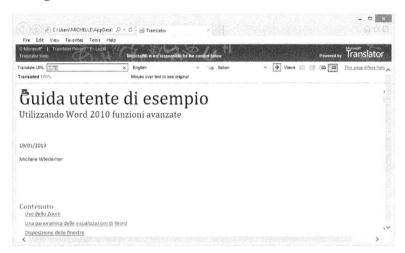

Step 5b: Select **Translate Selected text** to see a translation of just a few words. The Research task pane opens with the current translation settings and your translated text.

Step 6: Select **Mini Translator** to turn the Mini Translator option on or off. To use it, click a word in your document. The Mini Translator is slightly visible. To make it more visible, click it.

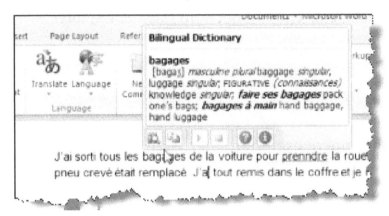

Setting Proofing Language and Language Preferences

To change the language, use the following procedure.

Step 1: Select the **Review** tab.

Step 2: Select **Language**. Select Set **Proofing Language**.

Step 3: Select the language you want to use from the *Language* dialog box and select **OK**.

To set Language Preferences in the Word Options dialog box, use the following procedure.

Step 1: Select **Language** from **Review** tab on the Ribbon.

Step 2: Select **Language Preferences**.

Step 3: In the *Word Options* dialog box, select the **Editing Language** you want to use for dictionaries, spell check and sorting.

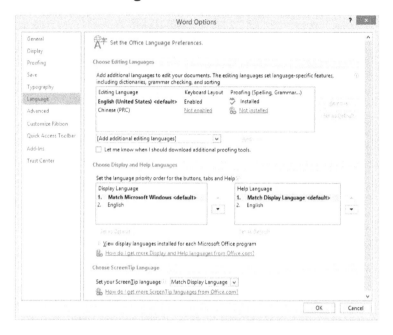

Step 4: Select **OK**.

Chapter 10 – Using Comments and Tracking

This chapter will explain how to review a document. You can add, reply to, or review comments. Comments are separate from the main text of the document. Track changes, on the other hand, allow you to make changes directly to the document in such a way that other reviewers can see your changes. Then you can review those changes and decide whether to keep them or not. Finally, this chapter explains how to compare different documents.

Adding a Comment

To add a comment, use the following procedure.

Step 1: Place the cursor where you want to mark a comment or highlight the portion of text on which you want to comment.

Step 2: Select the **Review** tab from the Ribbon.

Step 3: Select **New Comment**.

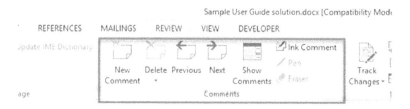

Word inserts a comment bubble with the Comments window open.

Step 4: Enter the comment text.

The Comment window closes when you click somewhere else in the document. You can also close it by clicking the X at the top right corner. To open it again, click the Comments bubble near the right margin.

To reply to a comment, use the following procedure.

Step 1: In the Comments window, click the Reply icon.

Step 2: Enter your text.

To review comments, use the following procedure.

Step 1: Select the **Review** tab from the Ribbon.

Step 2: Select **Show Comments**.

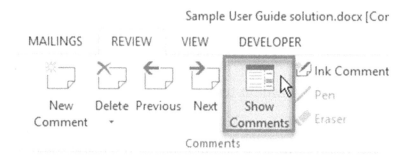

Step 3: Use the **Next** and **Previous** tools to move from one comment to the next.

Step 4: Review the comments in the Markup area.

To delete a comment, use the following procedure.

Step 1: Place your cursor anywhere in the selection for the comment you want to delete.

Step 2: Select the **Review** tab from the Ribbon.

Step 3: Select **Delete**.

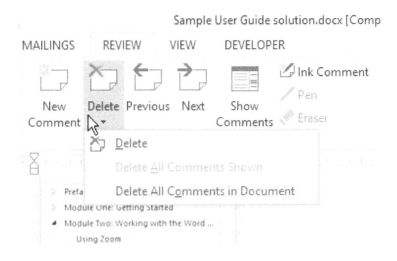

Tracking Changes

Use the following procedure to track changes.

Step 1: Select the **Review** tab from the Ribbon.

Step 2: Select **Track Changes**.

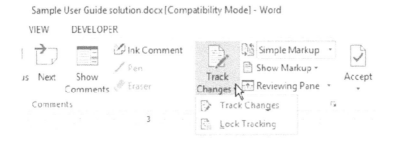

Step 3: Make edits to the document. Word places a line next to any area with changes. It marks insertions, deletions, moves, and formatting changes according to the settings in the *Change Tracking Options* dialog box.

However, you may not see all markups, depending on your settings.

> Show·the·participants·how·to·rearrange·the·sections·segments·in·a·document·using·the·Navigation¶
>
> {·XE·"Navigation"·}·pane.·Use·the·following·procedure.¶

Reviewing Changes

To open the Reviewing Pane, use the following procedure.

Step 1: Select the **Review** tab from the Ribbon.

Step 2: Select **Reviewing Pane**.

Step 3: Select the orientation you would like to use for the Reviewing pane.

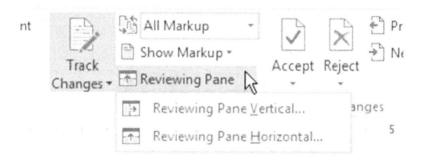

Word displays the Revisions Pane. The different authors who have made changes are indicated with a description of the change. When you click an item in the Revisions Pane, Word automatically scrolls to the corresponding location in the document.

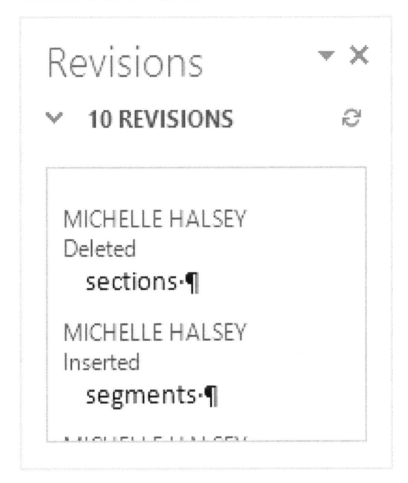

Select **Previous** or **Next** to move to another tracked change. Select **Accept** or **Reject** to accept or reject the current change.

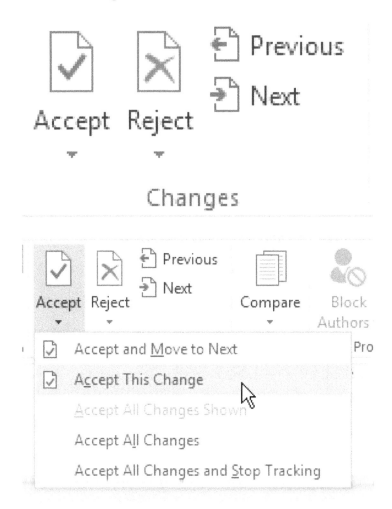

Comparing and Combining Documents

To compare documents, use the following procedure.

Step 1: Select the **Review** tab from the Ribbon.

Step 2: Select **Compare**. Select **Compare**.

Word opens the Compare Documents dialog box to determine which documents to use.

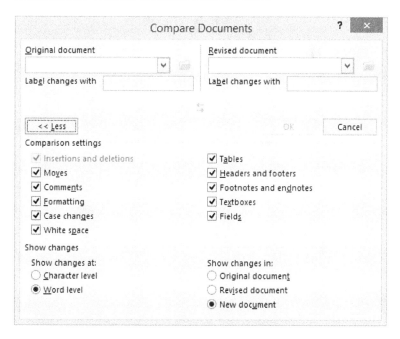

Step 3: Under **Original Document**, select the document considered the original from the drop down list. If the document is not listed, select the folder icon to navigate to the document and select **Open**. To label this document's changes, enter the label in **Label change with** field.

Step 4: Under **Revised Document**, select the document considered the revised document from the drop down list. If the document is not listed, select the folder icon to navigate to the document and select **Open**. To label this document's changes, enter the label in **Label change with** field.

Step 5: Select **More** to indicate which Comparison settings you want to mark. You can check or clear any of the boxes to control which items are compared. You can select whether to show changes at a character level or a word level. You can show changes in the **Original**, the **Revised** document, or a **New** document.

Step 6: Select **OK** to compare the documents.

Word compares the document. Note the Revisions pane, the Comparison document (in the middle), the original document (at the top right), and the revised document (in the bottom right) open in different panes.

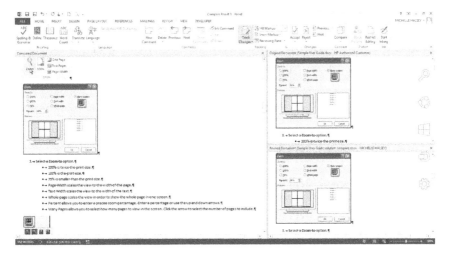

You will need to save the comparison document if you want to keep it.

The Combine documents process is the same procedure. If there are changes, Word can only store one set.

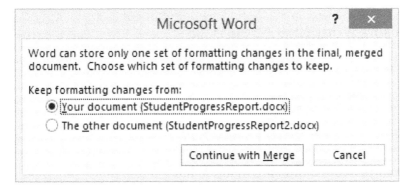

You will need to save the combined document if you want to keep it.

Additional Titles

The Technical Skill Builder series of books covers a variety of technical application skills. For the availability of titles please see https://www.silvercitypublications.com/shop/. Note the Master Class volume contains the Essentials, Advanced, and Expert (when available) editions.

Current Titles

Microsoft Excel 2013 Essentials

Microsoft Excel 2013 Advanced

Microsoft Excel 2013 Expert

Microsoft Excel 2013 Master Class

Microsoft Word 2013 Essentials

Microsoft Word 2013 Advanced

Microsoft Word 2013 Expert

Microsoft Word 2013 Master Class

Microsoft Project 2010 Essentials

Microsoft Project 2010 Advanced

Microsoft Project 2010 Expert

Microsoft Project 2010 Master Class

Microsoft Visio 2010 Essentials

Microsoft Visio 2010 Advanced

Microsoft Visio 2010 Master Class

Microsoft Access 2013 Essentials

Microsoft Access 2013 Advanced

Microsoft Access 2013 Expert

Microsoft Access 2013 Master Class

Microsoft PowerPoint 2013 Essentials

Microsoft PowerPoint 2013 Advanced

Microsoft PowerPoint 2013 Expert

Microsoft PowerPoint 2013 Master Class

Microsoft Outlook 2013 Essentials

Microsoft Outlook 2013 Advanced

Microsoft Outlook 2013 Expert

Microsoft Outlook 2013 Master Class

Microsoft Publisher 2013 Essentials

Microsoft Publisher 2013 Advanced

Microsoft Publisher 2013 Master Class

Windows 7 Essentials

Windows 8 Essentials

www.ingramcontent.com/pod-product-compliance
Lightning Source LLC
Chambersburg PA
CBHW070840070326
40690CB00009B/1630